BEI GRIN MACHT SICH IHR
WISSEN BEZAHLT

- Wir veröffentlichen Ihre Hausarbeit,
  Bachelor- und Masterarbeit

- Ihr eigenes eBook und Buch -
  weltweit in allen wichtigen Shops

- Verdienen Sie an jedem Verkauf

Jetzt bei www.GRIN.com hochladen
und kostenlos publizieren

Marriage and Family System among Bench People in South Western Ethiopia

Mamo Tsegaye

Bibliografische Information der Deutschen Nationalbibliothek:

Die Deutsche Nationalbibliothek verzeichnet diese Publikation in der Deutschen Nationalbibliografie; detaillierte bibliografische Daten sind im Internet über http://dnb.d-nb.de abrufbar.

ISBN: 9783346576989
Dieses Buch ist auch als E-Book erhältlich.

Druck und Bindung: Books on Demand GmbH, Norderstedt Germany
Gedruckt auf säurefreiem Papier aus verantwortungsvollen Quellen

Das vorliegende Werk wurde sorgfältig erarbeitet. Dennoch übernehmen Autoren und Verlag für die Richtigkeit von Angaben, Hinweisen, Links und Ratschlägen sowie eventuelle Druckfehler keine Haftung.

Das Buch bei GRIN: https://www.grin.com/document/1164850

Marriage and Family System among *Bench* People in South Western Ethiopia (Mizan)

By

Mamo Tsegaye

A Research Proposal Submitted to the Department of Social Anthropology in Partial
Fulfillment for the Requirements of Masters of Arts Degree in Social Anthropology

Department of Social Anthropology (MA)

College of Social Sciences and Humanities

Jimma University

December ,2019

Jimma, Ethiopia

1

Table of Contents

I. INTRODUCTION

1.1. Background of the Study

Ethiopia is a multi-ethnic country with over eighty five different ethnic groups and diverse cultural traits scattered throughout the country. Each ethnic group has their own cultural beliefs and practices that play a dominant role in shaping the behavior and action of its members. *Bench* people, as any other societies in Ethiopia, have their own forms of marriage and family system based on their culture. Families exist in all societies and they are part of what makes us human. However, societies around the world demonstrate tremendous variation in cultural understandings of family and marriage. Ideas about how people are related to each other, what kind of marriage would be ideal, when people should have children, who should care for children, and many other family related matters differ cross-culturally. Therefore, this study attempts to assess the marriage and family practices among *Bench* people.

Marriage and family are perhaps society's oldest institutions that are important for human existence. Although marriage and family are the foundation of human society and universal phenomena, these mutual institutions vary across cultures throughout globe. So many anthropologists and sociologists try to investigate and describe those socio cultural diverse styles that are present in many ethnic groups throughout globe to give acquittance for many people's those living in different continent of the world.

There are various conceptual perspectives that have been developed with respect to marriage and family, particularly with the notion that family is the entity responsible for the biological social reproduction. (cited in Ezra, Markos, 2003).

In Ethiopia the role of family is not limited to the sphere of biological reproduction and inter-generational solidarity. Families also play a crucial role as a production unit. More importantly family provides security in rural Ethiopia. This is true not only of emotional security, which so valued by other cultures, but also the security of survival and protection of the weak by the strong. The practice of these mutual institutions with in accepted norms and values of the society will provide greatest psycho- social satisfaction and valuable economic wealth. As it is the case with other societies, *Bench* societies has its own norms, customs, values, beliefs and cultural experiences that distinguish it from other societies. Since, multicultural practices in the society need comprehensive detailed studies.

3

Hence I was in this locality for more than seven years of my occupational placement and also as a member of society observed naturally the existing marriage and family system of *Bench* society in relation to the structure, forms of marriage, mate selection, marital arrangement, place of residence, and other related important family issues will be incorporated and represented through descriptive writing.

1.2. Statement of the Problem

Even though; some scholars have conducted anthropological and sociological studies on those multicultural practices in so many parts of the world including in Ethiopian societies way of life. The absence of well-trained domestic professional scholars and the scarcity of foreign scholars make difficulties to conduct comprehensive studies on diverse cultural practices of different ethnic groups in many parts of Ethiopia.

One of an adequately studied society in Ethiopia is the *Bench* society. In 2003, Hildebrand studies on economic, religion, language aspect of Bench ethnic groups. Morever, in 2009, individuals like Mirutse Gidaye,Zemede Asfaw,Zerihun Wolde,Tilahun T/haynot, attempt to studies on medicinal plan knowledge of this community. In 2013, individuals like Muluneh Tefera and Derge Tadesse studies on Ethno history of Bench people. Also in 2018 Adam Dagne studied on marital rights of women in *Bench* people. But these studies do not give comprehensive clue and do not address many aspects of marriage and family system of the people. Therefore, my research will attempt to asses and document the marriage and family aspect of *Bench* people. In doing so I will add ethnographic information of these people, as a result that will benefit many parties.

1.3. Objectives of the study

With the view to contribute to the solution to the above stated problems particularly problems related with the lack of detailed study on marriage and family system of Bench people, the research has aimed to address the following general and specific objectives

1.3.1. General Objective

- The overall objective of this study is to investigate the marriage practice and family system in Bench people.

1.3.2. Specific Objectives

To address the general objective of the study, the specific objectives are:

- To identify types of customary marriage practice s in *Bench* people;

4

- To understand the nature and practice of bride price payment among *Bench* people;

- To identify forms of family in *Bench* people;

- To identify socio economic role of marriage and family in *Bench* people;

- To investigate the family system network in *Bench* people;

- To explore the history, economic activities ,belief systems of *Bench* people;

- To examine the perception of *Bench* and the societal attitudes towards the customary practice of bride price.

1.4. Research Questions

To attain the above problem statement, this study is attempted to address the following research questions are formulated:

- What are the types of customary marriage practice in *Bench* society?

- What are the forms of families in *Bench* society?

- What are the socio economic roles of marriage in Bench society?

- What are the perception of *Bench* and the attitudes of the society towards bride price?

- How the family network system functioned in *Bench* society?

1.5. Scope of the Study

This study has both thematic and geographical delimitations depending on budget and scope of the study. Thematically, it assessed customary marriage practices of Bench people, types of marriage, kinds of marriage payment, the role marriage and family in the Bench people.

Geographically, the study is delimited to *Bench sheko* zone, in SNNPR on the selected two kebeles namely *Shasheqa* and *Hibret*.

The target group of the study (interview) is selected from both the rural and urban places which incorporated different areas engaged in marriage and also who are not engaged of males and females. It will focus on identification of the marriage and family aspects of the Bench community.

1.6. Significance of the Study

Conducting this study has been multiple significances for different target groups especially it will have practical and academic significance. Firstly, the main significance of this study is to give an insight to general understanding of marriage and family system of Bench society and also serves as a springboard for future in-depth research and expansion of the research to other areas.

It also gives local based relevant information for government and nongovernment bodies who are interested to work for any family life improving interventions programs.

II. LITERATURE REVIEW

2.1. General Overview of marriage

Many Anthropologists have proposed several competing explanations or definitions of marriage, so as to encompass the wide variety of marital practices observed across cultures. However probably there was no definition stretched and qualified, which can includes all societies and all the relationships that have been called marriage.

Marriage is emotional and commitment of two people to share emotional and physical intimacy, various tasks and economic resources (Defrain and Olson, 1999;p 8).

Also marriage is not only the emotion of men and women, but it can include same sex couples in same culture of the world (ibid).

Edward Westermarck, defines marriage as "socially legitimate sexual union, began with public pronouncement under taken with the idea of permanence, assumed with more or less explicit marriage contract which spells out reciprocal economic obligation between spouses and their future children's,(Westermarck 1921:71).

Bell describes marriage as "a relationship between one or more men (male or female) in severalty to one or more women that provides those men with a demand right of sexual access within a domestic group and identifies women who bear the obligation of yielding to the demands of those specific men(Bell 1997:38). Also Hobel(1966.32) defined marriage as a complex of social norms that defines and control the relation of a connubial pair to each other, their kin men , their offspring's and society at large. It defines all the institutional demand rights, duties, immunities, and so on of the pairs as husband and wife. It is the institution that shapes the form and activities of the association known to the family.

The type, function and characteristics of marriage vary from culture to culture, and can change over time in different societies. Generally there are two types of marriage in the world. These are civil and religious based.

In America and Europe in the 20th c legally recognized marriage are formally presumed to be monogamous. In these countries divorce is relatively simple and accepted among the society. In the west marriage has involved from the little life time covenant that can only be broken by fault or death to a contract that can be broken by either party at will. As any other societies of the world, in Ethiopia there are different ways through which marriage can be contracted (Buagiar, 1964 in Dagne 1995: 33). Under the civil code of Ethiopia, marriage is monogamous union, as religious practice it has always been in Christians Ethiopia; it is voluntary union of one man and woman to the exclusion of all other. The code ignores and even prohibits the polygamous which is the common forms of marriage among many of the ethnic groups of Ethiopia with such fundamental limitations in it; the code recognizes three (3) types of marriage namely: civil marriage, religious marriage and customary marriage.

2.1.1 Marriage rules

Being conventionally prescribed by the society, marriage rules are expected to be followed in the interest of the solidarity of the group. These rules are believed to be important since they aim at preventing inbreeding and encouraging maximum possible out breeding with the social norm (Jha 1999:82). Two general patterns of marriage rules exist: endogamy, marriage between people of the same social group or category; and exogamy, marriage between people of different social groups or categories (Scupin and Decorse 1995: 282; Jha 1999:69).

Other rules of marriage are cross cousin marriage, a marriage in which male marries a female who is hi fathers sisters daughter or his mother's brothers daughter(Scupin and Decorse2005:360;Jha 1999:82), and parallel cousin marriage , marriage in which a male marries his father's brothers daughters(Scupin and Decorse 2005:384-5).

2.1.2. Forms of marriage

The most common forms of marriage are monogamous and polygamous. Monogamous is a form of marriage in which one spouses of each sex or one woman and one man are married only to each other (Schafer 2003:350;Kottak 2005: 177; Scupin and Decorse 1995:281;Jha 1999;71). Polygamy (plural marriage) , which is marriage of one to many spouses ; it has two forms : polygyny, a type of marriage in which one man marry more than one woman or a man has more than one wife, and more rarely polyandry, a type of marriage in which a woman has more than one husband (Olson and Defrain 2000:50; Scupin and Decorse 1995:281). Also polyandry can be carried out in two forms. These are fraternal polyandry , a marriage in which brothers share a wife, and non-fraternal polyandry , a type of marriage in which non relatives share a wife or a woman marry more than one man but not necessarily brothers.

The other sub forms of marriage are levirate marriage or widow inheritance and sororate marriage or marrying deceased wife's sister (Jha 1999:74). Arranged marriage is in other word is a form of marriage in which families mostly choose their child's spouse; the reason was that youngsters are considered as un mature (Schafer 2003:537).

2.1.3 Functions of marriage

Marriage has several functions to the individuals as well as the whole community. According to Jha (1999:69-70) the four main function of marriage are as follows:

▪ **Social function:** the creation and perpetuation of the family, the formation of person-to-person relation and lining of one kin group to another kin group is possible through the institution of marriage.

▪ **Biological function:** human beings, like other animal species must mate so as to produce themselves. The sexual difference between human and other animal is that human beings tend to form relatively permanent mating pairs. This is made through marriage, which serves as a means for getting together to satisfy sexual needs and to found children(offspring's).

▪**Educational function:** with the institution of marriage that human infants who have the longest period of dependency get education through the process called enculturation, the process by which a child learns his or her culture; or in another way, the process by which culture is learned and transmitted across generations.

▪ **Economic function:** the institutions of marriage serve as an agent that performs economic function. It does this by bringing economic cooperation between men and women. This cooperation then leads in to survival of the society at large.

2.1.4. Marriage payment (bride wealth)

Bride wealth is any customary gift either in cash or kind before, at or after the marriage from the husband and his kind to the wife and her kin. Dowry is also the marital exchange in which the wife's family provides a sustainable gift to the husband's family; and this exchange is mostly practiced in India.

Bride service (the agreement by the groom to work for a time for the bride's family) are the main marriage payment known worldwide (Cherlin 2002:59, Scupin and Decorse 2005:434; Kotak 2005:174; Jha 1999:85-86).

Mostly the reason for bride wealth is considered as compensation to the bride's family for the loss of their right to her labor and children. The transfer of these rights between parties can be major economic and social importance. It establishes political networks and is commonly considered to the legal recognition of marriage and children (levinson and Ember, 1996:151).

Bride wealth may be some times exchange of woman with each other. Many parts of the world it is highly common in patrilineal   society with various ways according to the tribe.

2.2. General overview of family

Similarly as marriage, many anthropologists and sociologists define family in different ways.

Anthropologists define the family as a social group of two or more people related by blood, marriage, or adoption who live or reside together for an extended period, sharing economic resources and caring for their young (George,Murdock,1945). Family is two or more people who are committed to each other and who share intimacy, resource, decision making responsibility and values (Defrains,Olson,1999:8).

Like Murdock and Defrains explanation, family is also defined as any group of persons united by the ties of marriage, blood or adoption, or any sexually expressive relationships in which the adults cooperate financially for their mutual support and care of the children, the people are committed to one another in an intimate interpersonal relationship and the member see their identity as importantly attached to the group with an identity of its own (Rice, F,Philip, 1992:4).

2.2.1. Forms of family

The structures of family norms are various in different parts of the world. What the family constitute can changes on culture, tradition, wealth and mobility.

Construction of family can be done on the basis of the criterion of marriage based on the forms of marriage, family can be monogamous, polygynous and polyandrous family (Jha 1999:p.94).

Family can be constructed on the form of descent (the way in which one acquires membership of a kinship group as a criterion for classification. Based on this way there were patrilineal family, where its member's trace their ancestor through father; matrilineal family, members trace their ancestor through their mother's; bilateral family, its members trace their ancestors through both mother and father; ambilineal family, members trace their ancestors through in their father in one generation and in the next generation, one's son may trace his mother (Cherlin 2002:46-47;Schefer 2003:351; Jha1999:94-95).

The most common forms of family in the world are nuclear and extended family.

▪ **Nuclear family**: consists ofa father, mother and their children's all in one household dwelling. This kind of family is common where families are relatively mobile, as in modern industrialized societies. Usually there is a division of labor requiring the participation of both men and women. Nuclear family vary in the degree to which they are interdependent or maintain close ties to the kindred of the parents and to other families in general. Nuclear family is typically center on a married couple, but not always the family may have any number of children (Murdock, G, peter, 1965). It is composed of two parents and their immediate biological offspring's or adopted children (Jha,1999:97).

▪ **Extended family:** consists of husband and wife, their children's, and other members of either husband's or wife's family. This kind of family is common in cultures where property is inherited. In patriarchal societies where important property is owned by men, extended families commonly consist parents, children's and other kin relations bound together as a social unit. In societies where fathers are absent and mothers do not have the resource to rear their children on their own, the extended family may consist of a mother, and her children, and members of the mother's family (Cherlin 2002;Jha 1999), Rogers (1981:270) states that extended families are produced with patrilineal descent groups and also possible with matrilineal descent group. Extended family is merely likely to be found in the world with agrarian societies. Among its characteristics are exchange of information from experienced older members to less experienced young ones, care of the older family members in the home by the younger ones, and care of younger members children's' by older members.

2.2.2. Functions of family

Family is important to society, because it responds to some of the fundamental human needs, both individuals and collective. Murduck (1945) states that the primary function of the family is the nurturing and enculturation of children. The basic norms, values, knowledge's, and world views of the culture are transmitted to children through the family. Another function of family is the regulation of sexual activity.Family also serve to protect and support their members physically, emotionally and often economically from birth to death. In all societies people need warmth,food,shelter and care. Families provide social environment in which these needs can be met. Additionally, humans have emotional needs for affections and intimacy that are most easily fulfilled within the family.

Mostly, sexual cohabitation between spouses automatically leads to birth of offspring's. Hence, a society reproduces itself biologically through family (Jha 1999:93;Zerihun 2000:124).

III. THE RESEARCH METHODOLOGY

3.1. The Research Design

The study will be used descriptive method of research. The researcher will find this the most appropriate approach as this study will mainly employ gathering and classifying data from the selected population of the study. This type of research also utilizes interview, key informants, focus group discussion, observation and questionnaires in the study.

Descriptive research design is a scientific method which uses logical procedures to observe and describing the behavior, characteristics, attitude or opinion of the individuals, situation or phenomenon without influencing them in any way.

The research design for this study will be a Descriptive with qualitative research approach which generates data which will collect from select sample of respondents. This design will be select due to its suitability of describing the existing situation of any phenomenon.

By using this research design it has ensure, researcher will get the evidence which has answer the research questions.

3.2. Research Approach

- To undertake this particular study, the researcher will employ the qualitative research method with ethnographical research approach to explore and investigate the phenomenon of marriage practice and family system in Bench people.

As it is explained by Creswell (2007), exploration requires going deep into people"s day to day life, interactions and expression of past experiences that can better captured through gathering qualitative information. This research method is used for data collection, analysis and interpretation and it is also helped the researcher to have an in-depth understanding of the respondents take on during marriage and family practice.

3.3. The Study Area

- This study will be conduct in the in department of social anthropology and data was collected from Bench Sheko Zone town in two kebeles namely namely *Shasheqa* and *Hibret*. Researcher will be obtaining adequate data on marriage practice and family system in Bench people.

3.4. Population of the Study

It is in this population, the researcher chosen the representative for the whole population. For the purpose of this study, the populations involve the target group of the study (interview) is selected from both the rural and urban places which incorporated different areas engaged in marriage and also who are not engaged of males and females and also religious leaders of community and influential peoples . Sample as a smaller group of subjects drawn from the population in which a researcher is interest in gaining information and drawing conclusions. It involves a process where a researcher extracts from a population a number of individuals so as to represent adequately a larger group.

3.5.Data Sources

The research will use both primary and secondary data sources. Primary data will be gathered using interview, questionnaires, key informants, focus group discussions and observation of the situations in the study areas. And also secondary data will be collected from internet brows, books, published and unpublished journal articles will be used as a source of information to this study to frame the theoretical basis of the study.

3.6. Tools of Data Collection

The researcher   utilizes interview, focus group discussion, observation, participant observation and questionnaires in the study. Also other pertaining source of secondary data will be used as a tool for this study.

3.7. Ethical considerations

In this study, different ethical issues will be considered. Moreover, the respondents will be participated in the study based on their written informed consent during data collection. Furthermore, the identity of respondents will be concealed based on the principle of confidentiality during data analysis. The collected data will be analyzed honestly without data changing and the findings of the study will be reported honestly as well.

Generally, the ethical considerations which will be taken in to account (considered) to protect participants' rights in detail include:

- ✓ The researcher will follow the basic ethical principles of scientific research in the processes of data collection, data presentation and analysis. Therefore, the researcher is kept the confidentiality of the selected key informants and participants in most instances as per the interest of the informants of the research who prefer to stay confidential. The researcher will also ask the consent and interest of the participants and key informants to record their sound and capture their image during focus group discussion and in-depth-interview.

- ✓ Dignity, right to refuse to participate, right to no harm and right to service. Confidentiality will ensure at all levels by anonymity to respondents.

- ✓ Avoid plagiarisms,

3.8. Data analysis and interpretation

The data gathered using different instruments are, field notes, diaries, from this records the data is organized and presented using narrations that make ready for analysis. In analyzing qualitative data, the researcher will try to categorize the response to better understand the findings specifically thematic analysis have been employed in this particular study to meet the corresponding specific objectives.

IV. TIME AND BUDGET BREAK DOWN

4.1. Time break down

Table 1. Work plan for the proposal on **Marriage and Family System of Bench People in South Western Ethiopia(Mizan)** 2019.

No.	Activities	Responsible body	Time frame					
			Jan,	Febr,	March	April	May	June
1	Proposal development	Researcher	✓					
2	Pilot study	Researcher		✓				
3	Data collection	Data collector		✓	✓			
4	Data processing and analysis	Researcher			✓		✓	
6	Final thesis submission	Researcher						✓

4.2. Budget break down

Table 2: Budget plan for the proposal on **Marriage and Family System of Bench People in South Western Ethiopia (Mizan)** 2019.

No	Budget Item	Unit Price	Units	Total in Birr	Remarks
1.	Data collection	350 per day		2450	
2.	Data entry and coding	Clark		150	
3.	Questionnaire duplication	1.00birr		100	
4.	Papers	150	3	450	
5.	Duplicating paper	500	1	500	
6.	Printing	300	4	1200	
7.	Copying	400	4	1600	
8.	Stationery	300	1	300	
9.	**Sub total**			**7,400**	
	Contingencies	5000	1	5000	
	Total			**11,750**	

V. REFERNCES

- Bell, Duran(1997)."Defining marriage and Legitimacy" Current Anthropology 38(2); 237-254.
- Cherlin A.J.2002.Public and Private families.An Introduction. (Third ed) Mc Graw- Hill Companies, Inc, New York.
- Creswell, John W. Educational Research: *Planning, Conducting and Evaluating Quantitative and Qualitative Research.* 4thed. Pearson: 2012 .
- Dagne, S(1995).Marriage and Family system among the Gedeo of Southern Ethiopia, A.A.U.
- Defrain, J and David Olson (1999).Marriage and Family diversity and strength. New York: Mayfield publishing, co.
- Ezra, Markos(September 22,2003), Journal of Comparative Family Studies, Factors associated with Marriage and Family formulation process in Southern Ehthiopia.
- Hobel Adamson E. Anthropology: The study of Man New York: Mc Graw- Hill Book Company,1966.
- Jha.M(1999). An introduction to Social Anthriopology, 2nded.Vikas Publishing home, India.
- Kottack, C.P.2005. Mirror for Humanity. A concise introduction to Cultural Anthropology.(Fourth edition). Mc Graw-Hill Companies Inc,New York.
- Levinson D, and Ember Meluvin,eds,(1996). Encyclopedia of Cultural Anthropology. American Reference Publishing Company,Inc,vol.3.
- Murdock,George,1945."The common Denominator of Culture". In Ralphlinton,ed;The Science of Man in the World crisis, pp.123-42. New York: Columbia University press.
- Rice,F,Philip,1992. Intimate Relationship, marriage and families California:Mayfield Pub Co.
- Roger.K.(1981). Cultural Anthropology .United State: Canada.
- Schaefer,R.T,2003, Sociology. (Eight edition), Mc Graw-Hill Companies,Inc,New York.
- Scupin R, and Decorse C,R,1995.Anthropology.A global perspective.(Second edition). Prentice Hall of India. New Delhi.
- Westmarck,Edvard,(1921). The History of Human marriage(p.71).
- Zerihun Doda (2004). Introduction to Socio Cultural Anthropology Health Science students of higher learning institution in Ethiopia. Debub University.

BEI GRIN MACHT SICH IHR
WISSEN BEZAHLT

- Wir veröffentlichen Ihre Hausarbeit,
  Bachelor- und Masterarbeit

- Ihr eigenes eBook und Buch -
  weltweit in allen wichtigen Shops

- Verdienen Sie an jedem Verkauf

Jetzt bei www.GRIN.com hochladen
und kostenlos publizieren